ANGRY WITHOUT A CAUSE

A THOUGHT-PROVOKING LOOK AT GOD'S VIEW OF ANGER

By Raymond Force

Copyright © 2007 by Raymond Force.

All rights reserved. No part of this publication may be reproduced, stored in a retrieval system or transmitted, in any form, or by any means, electronic, mechanical, recorded, photocopied, or otherwise, without the prior permission of the copyright owner, except by a reviewer who may quote brief passages in a review.

Printed in the United States of America

ISBN: 978-1-4276-1988-4

CONTENTS

Introduction 7

Chapter 1 - Dad Said 10

Chapter 2 - Children 16

Chapter 3 - Your Spouse 28

Chapter 4 - The Church 34

Chapter 5 - Be Ye Angry 48

Chapter 6 - Sarcasm 54

Chapter 7 - So What's the Problem? . . . 57

Chapter 8 - Making Progress 82

Chapter 9 - Dealing With
              an Angry Person 114

To Charles Schafer.
Thanks for investing your life into mine.

INTRODUCTION

SURGERY

BEFORE A SURGEON MENDS a person's body, he must first EXPOSE that which needs mending. The first few chapters of this book are designed to do the same.

A skilled surgeon is able to cut without leaving any UNNECESSARY SCARS. It is my intention to do the same.

All surgeries that involve a knife are somewhat PAINFUL. Sorry, but if I am to succeed in helping you, then this book will have to duplicate similar feelings.

MY PROBLEM WITH ANGER

Before you dive into the next few pages, I would like to point out that I do not want to sound as if I am looking down on anyone as I pen these thoughts on paper (or should I say my laptop). As a matter of fact, I am simply trying to help others out of the same pit that I was once in myself. My problem with anger enslaved me in that it affected every aspect of my life. It affected my home, my spiritual temperature, my preaching, my confidence toward God, and my ability to succeed in life.

Someone once said that we preach best what we need to learn the most. If that is true, then this should be a rather remarkable book.

NO LACK OF INFORMATION

Although this is not a 300-page book with a multitude of footnotes, it does happen to be a compilation of my studies from the School of Hard Knocks. It is, in a sense, my thesis, and your response will decide my final grade. Just remember, good books are not measured by the yard, but by the pound, and it is not those that read many books that do well, as much as those that master a few!

In the day in which we live, we have more information at our fingertips than ever before, yet so little obedience to God. While we continue to bask in the age of enlightenment, many still seem to be groping in the darkness. The goal of this book, therefore, is not to simply give you a fistful of knowledge, but rather, to encourage genuine obedience to God.

Chapter One

DAD SAID

WHEN I WAS GROWING up, there was always one phrase that seemed to carry a lot of weight around our house. Whether we were in the midst of a heated argument or we simply wanted to get our own way, we would often say, "Dad said!" Sound familiar? This would not only give us the authority (at least in our eyes) to proceed with confidence, but it would also transfer a certain amount of responsibility for what we were about to either do, or say, to someone else. To tell the truth, I am about to do the same before I begin this chapter. That is to say, in Matthew 5, Jesus makes a statement that is so strong, I feel compelled to make sure that you understand I am not the originator of the next few thoughts.

In Matthew 5, Jesus preached a sermon that many have titled the "Sermon on the Mount." According to the content of Christ's sermon, His listeners seemed to be much like people living today. That is, they not only had a propensity to be outwardly religious, but they also felt that they were "pretty good" people because they had not committed too many "MAJOR SINS." Through this message, however, Christ taught that God was (and still is) EQUALLY concerned with the everyday vices with which people struggle.

Notice very carefully what Jesus taught in Matthew 5:21:

"Ye have heard that it was said by them of old time, 'Thou shalt not kill; and whosoever shall kill shall be in danger of the judgment':"

At this point, I believe we can see why Jesus was a master teacher. First of all, He is, in a good sense, setting the people up by stating a very obvious truth to His listeners. He did this by quoting one of the Ten Commandments, and I am sure that many of them were nodding their heads in agreement as He made this statement. Why? Well, if they were like most people today, they understood that those that commit murder are in danger of being judged by God.

In verse 27 of the same chapter, Jesus made a similar statement, but this time he was dealing with a different issue:

"Ye have heard that it was said by them of old time, Thou shalt not commit adultery:"

Jesus was telling His listeners nothing new. Again, He was quoting from the Ten Commandments, and I am certain that a good number of His listeners knew that those that committed adultery were in danger of experiencing God's judgment; however, and this is a HUGE HOWEVER, in verses 22 and 28, Jesus made two very SURPRISING STATEMENTS:

Vs. 21 - *"Ye have heard that it was said by them of old time, 'Thou shalt not kill; and whosoever shall kill shall be in danger of the judgment':"*

Vs. 22 - *"BUT I SAY UNTO YOU, that whosoever is ANGRY with his brother without a cause shall be in danger of the judgment ..."*

Vs. 27 - *"Ye have heard that it was said by them of old time, Thou shalt not commit adultery:"*

Vs. 28 – *"BUT I SAY UNTO YOU, that whosoever LOOKETH on a woman to lust after her hath committed adultery with her already in his heart."*

Are you catching the gist of what Jesus was saying? This is an incredible truth. Jesus was (don't miss this) placing the sins of unjustified anger and the lust of the eyes in the same categories as murder and adultery. Essentially, Jesus was teaching that, from God's point of view, those that are given to a spirit of anger and those that have lusted after another woman in their heart are JUST AS IN NEED OF THE FORGIVENESS OF SINS as those that have committed murder and adultery.

Now, let's remember that this is not some man's private interpretation. As a matter of fact, from just reading the passage, one can easily see that I am not spinning these verses. This segment of the "Sermon on the Mount" is clearly teaching that God is JUST AS concerned about the sins of our heart as he is our outward actions.

PLEASE DON'T MISS WHAT I AM ABOUT TO SAY. I believe that one of the greatest problems that we have in Christianity today is that our churches are overrun with good, moral people that believe the right things. All that being said, you might be thinking, "What's wrong with that?" Well, let's put it this way. I believe that we have a multitude of church members that believe they are faithful followers of Christ because they are faithful to church, willing to give financially, outwardly moral, and intellectually "in-line" with their church's statement of faith. They may struggle with some basic heart issues, but at least they're not guilty of committing any "major sins" like murder, adultery, idolatry, et cetera. The problem is that JESUS DID NOT ALLOW ANY ROOM FOR HIS HEARERS TO MINIMIZE THE SINS OF THEIR HEART, like anger (which, from God's perspective, can be equated to murder), lusting after another woman (which God specifically calls adultery), and covetousness or materialism (which God calls idolatry in Colossians 3:8).

I don't know about you, but this certainly takes the wind out of my sail when I think of criticizing others that I see on T.V. or in the newspaper that have committed some of those "big sins." It certainly causes me to realize that my "little sins" (like anger), are not so little any more in the sight of God. Does this sound pretty tough? Well, just remember: "Dad" said.

Chapter Two

CHILDREN

THEY'LL BELIEVE ANYTHING

ONE THING THAT I love about little children is that they will seemingly believe anything. You could tell your children that pigs live on the moon, and they would probably believe it since, up to the age of about four or five, all they really know about life is Mommy and Daddy and their toys. In their minds, we are the biggest, the strongest, and the smartest people they know.

It must also be understood, on the other hand, that a parent can abuse this trust. In other words, parents that are often frustrated and furious with their children do not realize that they are planting subtle thoughts within their minds. To be more precise, their children will eventually start to BELIEVE that they are as LOW and INSIGNIFICANT as they FEEL when their parents are angry at them. Eventually, their minds will succumb to the silent, yet destructive messages that their feelings of inferiority are sending to them; hence, if it is your custom to regularly use hot demands, sarcastic remarks, temper tantrums, and frustrated phrases as a form of control over your children, you will not produce the healthy, well-balanced children that, deep down, you desire to have.

BEWARE

Proverbs 22:24-25 touches on the topic of anger:

"Make no friendship with an angry man; and with a furious man thou shalt not go: LEST THOU LEARN HIS WAYS . . . "

First off, these verses are clearly teaching that if anyone closely associates with an angry person, then that particular individual will eventually start to pick up some of their bad habits. If this is true concerning a friend that someone may only see a few days a week, then how much more applicable is this principle for children living in the same house as an angry parent?

Parents, although this is a very sobering thought, you must be aware that if you are consistently submitting yourself to a spirit of anger, then your children will inherit the tendency to do the same. Furthermore, by constantly giving in to this temptation, you are not only affecting your own children, but also the lives of your children's children and their spouses.

I am a firm believer that there is nothing magical about the wedding altar. If you allow certain faults and mistakes to be prevalent in the lives of your children, they will also take those same faults with them into their future marital relationship. This is why THE GREATEST TIME TO HAVE AN EFFECT UPON YOUR GRANDCHILDREN IS WHILE YOU ARE STILL REARING YOUR OWN CHILDREN.

One day, you will sit back as a grandparent or a concerned in-law and either grieve or rejoice over the relationship that your children have with their immediate family. The time for you to begin working on those relationships is now, while your children are still young and teachable, and not married to a person that may take offence at your advice.

There was once a country church that was having a Bible study. During that study, the attendees started discussing the proper age to start disciplining children. Some said, "When the child is two years old," while others chimed in by saying, "When he reaches the age of about three or four." Finally, an old woman in the back lifted up her hand and said, "Twenty years before the child is born." The old woman's answer resounded with truth. The way we train one generation has a dramatic effect upon the next.

UNJUSTIFIED ANGER

My best material on parenting seems to come from hanging out at Wal-mart or any local retail store. On more than one occasion, I have either hidden behind a manikin or pretended to look at something longer than I needed in order to witness a less-than-Biblical approach to parenting. More often than not, I have observed that parents are unjustifiably using anger to correct their children.

Let's take a moment to review a common scenario that takes place in many homes today. Imagine yourself working at your computer when one of your children starts to bang on the computer table with his Fisher Price hammer or her brand new baby doll. How do you react? Many parents do the following:

The parent says, "Stop that."

The child turns his head, but ignores the command and keeps banging away.

After about 30 seconds, the parent says something like "Hey, stop that."

The child may stop for a little while, but soon continues.

Then the parent angrily says, "Hey, didn't I say to stop doing that?!"

The child looks at the parent and goes and plays with something else for about a minute, but ends up coming back to continue his construction (or destruction) project.

Now, with a more frustrated tone of voice, the parent yells, "Stop that Johnny!"

Once again, the child continues.

Finally, the parent stomps over to the child and pulls the hammer out of his fingers and says angrily, "Can't you listen? I TOLD YOU FIVE TIMES TO STOP THAT!"

There are a few problems with this scenario. First of all, children that are subjected to this type of parenting subconsciously learn that Dad and Mom's first command means absolutely nothing. There is a saying, (I'm not sure where it originated), concerning civil law. It goes something like this:

"Laws are only as good as the men and women that enforce them."

As far as parenting is concerned, the same is also true. Only those parents that consistently back up their commands in a calm and confident manner, and the FIRST TIME their children disobey, are teaching them that their commands carry some type of weight.

Secondly, the parent's anger was unjustified, in that the attempt at disciplining did not have the good of the child in mind. Let's face it. The only reason the parent finally took decisive action was because the child finally infringed upon the parent's leisure time and comfort level enough to irritate him/her into taking action. This is what I call SELFISH-DISCIPLINING. This does nothing to teach the child how to properly respond to authority, nor does it help the child to properly obey in the future.

Before I conclude this portion of the book, I would like to add that parents' anger toward their children is also unjustified when the parents are upset at the children for behaving the way that they would be behaving if the PARENTS were trained by THEMSELVES. Was that a little wordy? Well, let me explain it like this. If a basketball coach neglects to practice with his players and teach them the fundamentals of the game, does he have a right to get mad at his players for playing poorly? If he ignores his responsibility to teach them the correct way to pass, shoot, and execute plays, will he have a right to become furious with them when they fail to perform during a game? The answer is obvious. In the same way, parents that abandon their responsibility to properly instruct and train their children have little right to become aggravated at them when they disobey at the mall, at school, or especially in front of the in-laws. We have a little saying around our house concerning this very same topic:

> "When our children embarrass us in public, then it is time to go home and train them in private."

Though it's not very catchy, it certainly keeps us from welling up with pride at the grocery store and acting in an irrational manner.

HOME MISSIONS

Look at what Charles Finney, the great American Evangelist of the 1800's, said in relation to parenting:

> "Parents should begin at the outset to get the mastery over the will [of their children] and then keep it. The most steadfast and uniform perseverance is essential to retaining the mastery of their will . . . IF I

FIND A PERSON LINGERING UNDER CONVICTION AND FINDING IT VERY DIFFICULT TO SUBMIT TO GOD . . . I OFTEN MAKE INQUIRY, AND WITH SCARCELY A SOLITARY EXCEPTION, FIND THAT PARENTAL AUTHORITY HAS NEVER HAD A THOROUGH INFLUENCE OVER HIM: his will was not early subdued, and ever after, while still a minor, he was not kept in a state of unqualified submission and obedience."

This is one amazing quote, and in my mind, it certainly explains why the primary role of Elijah, according to Malachi 4:6, will be to "*turn the hearts of the fathers to the children.*" In His infinite wisdom, God is fully aware that if parental authority is established in the home, then by the time children reach adulthood they will have an easier time submitting to their Divine Authority.

One of the things that I love about Biblical parenting is the freedom that it offers from yelling, screaming, and raising your voice in order to get your children to obey. It was such a blessing when my wife and I realized that children could be brought under subjection by using calm and confident commands. It was even more of an eye-opener for us to see that when you train your children to properly respond to authority, you are also accomplishing a much higher and nobler objective. You are not only increasing your chances of having a joyful atmosphere in the home, but you are also conditioning your children's hearts to one day properly respond to the "*STILL SMALL VOICE*" of the Holy Spirit.

If a child only learns to obey when his parents finally blow up or get belligerent with him, the child's heart is not being CONDITIONED to properly respond to the quiet prompting and prodding of the Holy Spirit of God. As a matter of fact, this type of child will often turn into an adult that will only respond to God after He has had to do something drastic or dramatic in his life in order to get his attention.

Parents, may I make a very pertinent statement at this time? Will the "*still small voice*" of the Holy

Spirit be a foreign language to your children because of the constant use of angry words, sarcastic remarks, and frustrated phrases in your home? Are you making the Holy Spirit's job more difficult because you have been attempting to control your children through harsh words and angry tones? May I say that we must not forget that God has given each and every parent a great mission field within the context of their own family. Dads and Moms, this "parenting-thing" is not just about learning some tips and techniques to keep your children out from "underneath your feet." Actually, you have an opportunity everyday to prepare the way of the Lord in the hearts of your children by teaching them to properly respond to Godlike authority.

Chapter Three

Your Spouse

LADIES FIRST

THE WOMAN THAT RIDICULES her husband by making sarcastic remarks and subtle inferences to his lack of leadership and abilities is not only hurting her husband, but also herself. She is not only ensuring that he will have a tough time rising above her low view of him, but she will also end up DESPISING HIM FOR NOT BEING HALF THE MAN THAT SHE HAS DISCOURAGED HIM TO BE. Deep within, she will struggle with feelings of contempt, since she longs for a man to look up to, but not a man that will look down on her. The problem is that by displaying her inner frustrations toward him, she has become her own archenemy. With her cross looks and her deep sighs, she helps to dig a pit for him that will eventually cause her to become more and more disgusted at his lack of ability to crawl out of it.

Throughout time, women have been tempted to withhold their love and affection toward their husbands because they fail to measure up to their expectations. A woman that has given in to this temptation must realize that when she holds back from loving her husband because he doesn't meet her standards, she is simply holding her love as a ransom until he comes up with the appropriate payment. This is actually a form of manipulation. It is not what she signed up for when she said, "I do."

No bride stands at a wedding alter and says, "I will love, honor, and adore you when you measure up to my expectations." It doesn't happen. That would be ridiculous. Most of the attendees to the wedding would be thinking, "I'd better keep my receipt." On the other hand, how many wives are living this out on a consistent basis? That's why, in our day and age, many go away from a wedding holding their breath and thinking, "This sure is a lot of money to spend for something that may not last more than a few years."

Ladies, you signed up to love him for better or for worse. Right now you may feel like it can't get any worse, but you must not be enticed to express your frustrations in an inappropriate fashion.

Carefully read the following letter that was written to a well known Christian counselor by the name of Clyde Narramore. I hope it will be a tremendous blessing to you. It's one of my favorite quotes on this subject.

> "One day, I was saved and I began to know what God could do for me. Was love something that you felt? Was it something that happened to you, or was it an act of the will?
>
> I finally faced the fact that I might not be able to feel love, but what I could do was

show forth love. From that moment on I began to behave as if I did feel love.

'What would I do for my husband today?' I asked myself, if I were really in love with him? Then I proceeded to do these little kindnesses.

I studied his likes and dislikes and bought little treats for his lunch box. I tried to comfort him when he came home from work, tired or harassed by a heavy schedule. I met him at the door with a smile. I respected his discipline of the children and worked with him. I tried to speak softly and diplomatically when we had differences. I listened to him.

Soon I noticed a marked change in him. He was behaving as though he were living with a woman who loved him. I began to notice a change in my own feelings. He was not at all like I had concluded. He had real depth, and I was beginning to fall in love with him." (1)

MOUNTAIN CLIMBING

I often tell people that there are three things that married couples argue about the most: Money, children, and physical intimacy. Men, if you are interested in excelling in the area of physical intimacy, you may want to carefully read the next couple of paragraphs.

Physical intimacy has been designed to be a physical expression of what has been going on all day long between a man and a woman. I often tell people that it is the top of the mountain that you begin to climb at the beginning of a day with your spouse. Men, you start that ascent by serving your wife, helping with the housework and the children, organizing a romantic getaway, calling her just for the sake of calling her, and speaking and acting kindly toward her. It should be noted that nothing aggravates a woman more than when her husband comes home and speaks rudely, neglects to connect with her and the children, watches TV for three or four hours, and about 10 P.M. says to his wife, "Hey, how about it?" If your wife is not emotionally involved with you, then she will typically have a difficult time being physically involved.

As far as anger is concerned, a man cannot speak in a harsh and cutting way toward his wife and expect her to undergo an EMOTIONAL METAMORPHOSIS between 10:30 and 11 PM. Generally speaking, it just doesn't happen. Romance may start for you at 10 P.M., but for her it starts at 10 A.M.

I think raising boys is a little easier than girls, in that boys tend to pout less and shake their hurt feelings quicker than girls. I grew up with three brothers and no sisters. I did not know this when I "tied the knot," but girls tend to take things more personal than boys. When I was growing up, my brothers could be "duking it out" one minute, and having an intense, yet enjoyable game of basketball the next. My four daughters do not seem to have the same capability. Needless to say, neither does my wife. Come to think of it, neither do most females.

Chapter Four

The Church

WORLDLINESS

I HAVE FOUND THERE ARE some Christians that believe they are different from the world because of the mere fact that they have changed the social places they frequent, their language, their dress, and the type of entertainment they enjoy. Christians that fall into such a category should be complimented for their zeal to forsake anything they would consider to be displeasing to God in their lives. However, I believe it is safe to say that they have fallen short of what God expects of them, if they have not

ALSO taken the time to deal with INTERNAL sins, like anger, bitterness, and pride, et cetera.

In Colossians 3:5-8, the Apostle Paul took time to describe to the church at Colossae some sinful habits that were in their lives when they were "out in the WORLD" and without Christ. I believe he was attempting to teach them that although these sinful behaviors were once in their lives before they came to Christ, now, these WORLDLY ways should be laid aside. Carefully read the words of the Apostle Paul in Colossians 3:5-8:

> *"Mortify therefore your members which are upon the earth; fornication, uncleanness, inordinate affection, evil concupiscence, and covetousness, which is idolatry: For which things' sake the wrath of God cometh on the children of disobedience: In the which ye also walked some time, when ye lived in them. But now ye also put off all these; anger, wrath, malice, . . ."*

Many times, when Christians think of coming

"out of the world," they tend to concentrate on outward actions and deeds. The Apostle Paul did not limit the concept of worldliness to these. As a matter of fact, when he commanded the church of Colossae to forsake their worldly ways, he did not deal simply with the sins of the flesh. He also addressed sins of the heart, the mind, and the spirit. One of the sins that he brought to their attention was ANGER.

Have you ever considered that if you are consistently given to anger after becoming a Christian, then there is WORLDLINESS or WORLD-LIKE-NESS that is still in your life? Have you ever realized that when you "lose it" with your children, and when you are cross with your spouse, you are giving into a world-like spirit?

Pastors and lay leaders, if the people in your church are consistently displaying their anger toward one another and the leadership of the church, then you must admit that you are dealing with a body that has some worldly ways to overcome. This is actually what the Apostle Paul said to the Corinthian church in I Corinthians 3:3:

"For ye are yet carnal [earthly or worldly]: for whereas there is among you envying, and strife, and divisions, are ye not carnal, and walk as men?"

Paul didn't "sugarcoat" the issue. He didn't think of these believers as good Christian people with some personality problems. He clearly stated that they were acting in a carnal or a worldly manner.

In one of my pastorates, I found myself consistently dealing with people that were angry at one another and the decisions that were made by the leadership of the church. I don't know if any of you have ever witnessed this before, but the only time the people seemed to be unified was when they were all upset at the same person. Interestingly enough, the majority of my problems came from some of the most faithful people in the church. They were rather religious, but, according to the

Bible, they were also rather worldly. With all my heart, I believe that this type of worldliness is what is hurting the church more than anything else, and the only way we are going to begin to combat it is by calling it what it really is . . . worldliness.

THE BLESSINGS OF GOD

The most common mistake I see pastors making is to think that a certain style of music, a particular style of dress, a specific evangelistic program, or a lack (or abundance) of technological advancements in their church is the key to securing the blessings of God.

I have met some pastors that feel their church needs to be the church of the future in order to prosper, whereas, others are adamant that their congregation must be the church of the past. May I be candid here? If any pastor thinks that the Holy Spirit is looking to bless one particular style, then he is mistaken. According to the scriptures, THERE IS ONLY ONE THING THAT KEEPS THE BLESSINGS OF GOD FROM

PERMEATING A CHURCH. The answer can be found in II Corinthians 6:16-17:

". . . for ye are the temple of the living God; as God hath said, I will dwell in them, and walk in them; and I will be their God, and they shall be my people. Wherefore come out from among them and be ye separate, saith the Lord, and touch not the unclean thing; and I will receive you."

Let's ask ourselves a very simple question. What truths are obvious from these two scriptures? First of all, we can see that God desires to supernaturally bless His church with His POWER and His PRESENCE.

Secondly, this portion of chapter six teaches us that God will only manifest Himself to a people that are considered HOLY in His sight.

II Corinthians 7:1 seems to summarize what the Apostle Paul wrote in verses sixteen and seventeen of chapter six. However, this particular verse deals with the matter in a more specific manner. II Corinthians 7:1 says:

> *"Having therefore these promises [the promise of His presence and His power], dearly beloved, let us cleanse ourselves from all filthiness of the flesh and spirit . . ."*

This is an awesome scripture! First off, notice that this verse says: *"Having therefore these promises."* Now, we need to ask, "What promises?" And we see that the answer has already been revealed in verses sixteen and seventeen of chapter six. God is promising to bless the church with HIMSELF.

Secondly, II Corinthians 7:1 states that if the church wants to be blessed with God and all that comes with Him, then it must be willing to cleanse itself *"from all filthiness of the flesh AND SPIRIT . . ."*

I strongly believe that, in reality, the following rendition of II Corinthians 7:1 is what many churches and church leaders are living out today:

> *"Having therefore these promises [the promise of His presence and his power], dearly beloved, let us refrain from making any technological advancements, cling to our hymnals, preserve our pews, and live in the past."*

Or:

> *"Having therefore these promises [the promise of His presence and his power], dearly beloved, let us buy a power point projector, dress casual, use the wall as our hymnal, throw out the pews, and preach 10 minute sermons."*

[By the way, before I go any further, please keep in mind that I love most of the old hymns and I'm not afraid of a song because it is new. I'm okay with chairs, pews, power point, ties, and turtlenecks.]

Invariably, the most common conversation I have with pastors goes something like this:

Me: "How's your church doing?"

Pastor: "It's going alright, but I don't feel that the church is where I want it to be. I'm hoping to be able to start introducing a few of the newer songs and maybe get a guitarist or two in here."

Or:

Me: "How's your church doing?"

Pastor: "It's going alright, but I don't feel that the church is where I want it to be. I just heard about a new program that I think might inspire our people to invite more people to church. I hope it works."

Or:

Me: "How's your church doing?"

Pastor: "It's going alright, but I don't feel that the church is where I want it to be. I'm hoping that my deacons won't put up too much of a fuss about my idea to buy a power point projector and a screen for behind the pulpit. You know, we've got to find a way to keep the young people around here."

I believe the focus is so off in our modern day church setting. No, I'm not against using different methods or introducing new programs, but the real question is, "WHERE IS OUR PRIMARY FOCUS?" According to II Corinthians, it should be on our spiritual condition before God. In other words, GOD IS NOT INTO STYLE, HE'S INTO SPIRITUALITY, and it should be understood that the Holy Spirit will not be manipulated by our carnal attempts to procure the blessings of God in the church:

At this time you may be thinking to yourself, "What does this have to do with anger?" Well, did you notice that when Paul taught on the subject of holiness in II Corinthians 7, he did not simply deal with the sins of the body. He also addressed the sins of the spirit, and, of course, we know from previous chapters that we can include anger as one of these sins.

Churches can change their programs, their style

of music, their service times, and their dress, or they can keep them the same. It must be said, however, that if a church is not diligently dealing with the element of sin in the body, then the Holy Spirit simply sees angry, covetous, and faithless people that have either saved or sunk their traditions.

THE TONGUE

We are all well acquainted with anger. Though it is seldom our friend, it knows no strangers. As a result, after coming to Christ, many new believers are bringing this unwelcome guest with them into the church. To the dismay of their respective pastors and spiritual leaders, it has a way of lying low until it crosses paths with what I view to be normal, unavoidable conflict. Unfortunately, the tongue becomes the medium through which this anger is expressed.

THE AVERAGE CHURCH NEEDS INCREDIBLE REFORM IN THE AREA OF HANDLING CONFLICT. In Luke 17:3, Jesus said:

"If thy brother trespass against thee, rebuke him . . ."

He did not say:

"If thy brother trespass against thee, go to another brother and tell him how much you would like to rebuke the brother that offended you."

Sadly to say, I have observed that, in many (if not most) churches, the made up verse is the normal scenario that people follow for handling conflict. In Matthew 18:15, Jesus explicitly taught that if someone has offended you, that you are to go and talk to that person alone. I am a firm believer that this is one of the most DISOBEYED commands in the church today.

God is very concerned about the words that we speak. Carefully read what I think is one of the strongest verses in the Bible:

James 1:26: *"If any man among you seem to be religious, and bridleth not his tongue, but deceiveth his own heart, this man's RELIGION IS VAIN."*

From observation, I believe it's safe to say that our churches are heavily saturated with faithful, active church members that consistently speak in a way the Bible would deem as inappropriate. According to James, no matter how much they attend church, work in the church, or even enjoy church, in the eyes of God, their "Christianity" is of a low quality. Does this sound pretty tough? Well, it would do us good at this point to recall the words of Jesus in Matthew 12:34. In this passage, Christ said:

". . . out of the abundance of the heart the mouth speaketh."

Christ was teaching that people reveal what is in their hearts by what comes out of their mouths. If they are full of a spirit of love, joy, peace, and gentleness, et cetera, that is what will consistently come from their lips. On the other hand, if they are filled with anger, bitterness, a negative outlook on life, jealousy, and a critical spirit, then that is exactly what will proceed from their lips.

THE MISUSE OF THE TONGUE IS THE GREATEST KILLER OF CHURCHES TODAY. If I went to the average church and conducted a survey from the pulpit, I believe the results would be predictable. If I asked people in most congregations, how many have personally been a part of a church that has been destroyed because of the misuse of alcohol, I may not see many hands go up. If I asked how many have been a member of a body that has been destroyed or severely hurt because of adultery, about ten to twenty percent might raise their hands. But if I asked how many have, with their own eyes, witnessed the destruction of a congregation due to the misuse of the tongue, more than half, if not most, of the hands in the auditorium would be in the air. To me, this is proof positive that the church must begin to consistently exalt a Biblical standard in this area.

Chapter Five

BE YE ANGRY

WHEN A PERSON FEELS angry inside, are they ALWAYS sinning against God? Well, if that was the case, then God Himself would be a sinner. In Psalm 7:11, the Bible teaches us that "*God is angry with the wicked every day.*" On many occasions in the scriptures, the Bible states that "the anger of the Lord was kindled" against certain individuals and nations. In Mark 3:5, the Bible tells us that Jesus "*looked around about them [the Pharisees] with anger.*" Obviously, since God is completely holy and without sin, anger can actually, at times, be a HOLY EMOTION.

May I make what may be a rather surprising statement to you? In the book of Ephesians, the Bible actually COMMANDS us, under certain situations and circumstances, to be angry. Look at the words of the Apostle Paul in Ephesians 4:26:

"Be ye angry, and sin not . . ."

I believe one of the best examples of an individual in the Bible that was feeling the type of anger mentioned in this verse can be found in the thirty-second chapter of Exodus. In Exodus 32, we find a man called Moses returning to the camp of the Israelites after spending time with the Lord. The Bible reveals to us that when Moses returned to the camp, he found his followers worshiping a golden calf. In response to this, Moses became angry. In fact, Exodus 32:19 tells us that when Moses saw the golden calf, his "*anger waxed hot.*"

Let me ask a more than relevant question at this point. Was Moses sinning against God by allowing his emotions to get into such a condition? I do not believe so. As a matter of fact, I believe that we can learn a major lesson from this account. Moses' primary reason for becoming angry was that he was grieved over the fact that the children of Israel were committing the sin of idolatry. Moses became enraged because God's reputation and the spiritual welfare of the people of God were at stake. In this particular instance, God not only allowed Moses to experience these emotions, but I believe He expected it.

Let me interject a rather thought provoking statement. IT IS IMPOSSIBLE TO LOVE SOMETHING OR SOMEONE WITHOUT HATING THAT WHICH WOULD POTENTIALLY DO THAT SOMETHING OR SOMEONE SERIOUS HARM. Moses' love for God's name and God's people was what provoked his intense feelings. In a day when many are labeling those that are intolerant toward the moral debauchery of our times as hate-mongers, it is important to realize that some of our more intolerant members of the church and our society are actually very LOVING PEOPLE. That is, their love for God, the truth, the church, their family, and their country is what inspires their intolerance.

Before closing this section, I would like to confess that within my heart is a fear that some may take the information expressed in this segment and run in a direction that is potentially dangerous. I say this because throughout my ministry, I have met Christians that seemed to be saved and mad about it instead of saved and glad about it. It's as if, after they came to Christ, they simply started to ride a horse of a different color. That is, they still had the same spirit of anger in their hearts that they possessed before coming to Christ, but after coming, they seemed to justify their negativity by quoting Bible verses and tacking the name of God to their issues. It was as if they spent much of their devotional life in the book of Lamentations. Because of this danger, I would like to take some time to give you some ways to differentiate between righteous and unrighteous anger:

1. Righteous anger causes people to stick with the facts. Unrighteous anger inspires people to revert to name calling, belittling, et cetera.
2. Righteous anger causes people to deal with real issues; whereas, unrighteous anger provokes people to make their case based on assumption.

    Many times, we like to assume things that are not actually present in a situation because our angry spirits cause our minds and emotions to be like children at an amusement park. They are frantically looking for something to ride.
3. Righteous anger does not prohibit you from exhibiting the fruits of the Spirit, like love, joy, peace, longsuffering, meekness, and SELF-CONTROL. Unrighteous anger will ensure that you are bitter, tense, rude toward others, and OUT OF CONTROL.
4. Righteous anger will cause you to desire that others experience a genuine sense of conviction over their sin. Unrighteous anger

produces feelings of inferiority in other people.

5. Righteous anger inspires individuals to address cores issues. Unrighteous anger focuses on petty issues.

6. Righteous anger tends to produce a belief system that promotes a well-balanced Christian life. Unrighteous anger drives people toward unhealthy extremes (even in the name of God).

7. Righteous anger inspires people to handle conflict in a Biblical manner. Unrighteous anger usually leads to gossip and unfruitful conversations about others.

Chapter Six

SARCASM

SARCASM IS SIMPLY A subtle way of venting our frustrations toward others. It discourages unity, closes spirits, and eats away at the emotional integrity of our homes. It does little to make ourselves, our faith, and our God attractive to those closest to us (especially our children), and though it is often senseless, it seems to be a widely accepted form of communication. In high school, I learned that sarcasm is one of the seven elements of humor. Funny thing, I've seldom seen the humor in cutting remarks that wound people's spirits and hurt a person's self-esteem.

There are a few verses that are quoted around our house more than others. Ephesians 4:29 is one of them. In this verse God gives us a very practical command concerning the words that we speak. It says:

"Let no corrupt communication proceed out of your mouth, but that which is good to the use of edifying . . ."

In this verse the Bible is clearly teaching us that God desires our words to edify one another. The word "edify" is closely associated with the word "edifice." Of course, we often use this word when we are talking about a building or a structure. When the Bible commands us to communicate in an edifying way, it is teaching us that we are to build one another up. Sarcasm does little to help us fulfill this command. Like termites, our sarcastic comments toward other people slowly, yet surely, eat away at their emotional and mental wherewithal.

We have a rule in our home. It is a little wordy,

but I think you will get the point. It goes like this:

Sarcasm is not allowed.

Chapter Seven

So What's the Problem?

THERE ARE SOME SUBJECTS I speak on that seem to consistently command the audience's undivided attention. These subjects include business, lust, worry, and last, but certainly not least, anger. The purpose of this entire chapter is to help us determine why we tend to struggle so much with this incredibly destructive vice.

HUMAN NATURE

My wife and I have five children. Not one of them has a laid-back personality. When they were toddlers, every one of them tried to get their way by either stomping their feet or arching their backs and throwing themselves upon the ground. When our first child tried this, we were convinced that it was because we were doing something wrong as parents. Now that we have a little experience under our belts, we understand that it is very natural for a child to manifest a spirit of anger. In fact, they have inherited this tendency from their great, great, great, great, great, great . . . grandpa Adam.

Even though anger is a natural emotion for us to experience, we should NEVER become too COMFORTABLE with its presence in our lives. Marijuana is a NATURAL substance, but this does not mean that the use of it is necessarily beneficial to our bodies and/or our minds. Tornadoes, hurricanes, and thunderstorms are natural phenomenons, but, like anger, their effects are too destructive for us to take lightly.

ANGER WORKS

Sorry, but it's true. The "squeaky wheel" is very good at getting "the grease." Businesses often give discounts and credits to customers that get irate, special interest groups impassioned by an angry spirit often make tremendous strides in the political realm, and children that are consistently throwing fits and venting their frustrations often do so because they have found it helps their cause.

It could be that you were from a home that either tolerated anger or facilitated your problem with anger. If so, then you may have developed the mind set that anger works. It is entirely possible you have subconsciously learned that an outburst of anger can sometimes work to your advantage. The problem is that even though your anger may help you get our own way, it seldom helps you feel closer to God or those that are closest to you. At times anger may work, but it certainly does not work very well.

DON'T GET IN MY WAY

It's entirely possible that you were born into a fairly functional home, you had a descent relationship with your father, and you were never physically, sexually, or verbally abused, yet you still struggle with the very thing that this book is talking about. It's also feasible there are no deep, unresolved issues from your childhood that are keeping you from calmly dealing with life's everyday problems, except for maybe one.

It could be that when you wake up in the morning, you are supremely focused on one thing – yourself. Your primary concern is your goals, your schedule, your needs, or your wishes. Your main goal in life is to please yourself and to do it as QUICKLY as possible. If anyone in your home dares to become a HUMAN SPEED-BUMP in your path, then you become agitated.

Early in our marriage, I was really into me. I had a horrible addiction. I was addicted to myself. I was saved, in church, and serving in the ministry, but I was supremely focused on me, and I was not very thrilled with anyone else that wasn't interested in the same.

I was not a fountain, but rather, I was a drain to those around me. Especially my wife. I withdrew much more than I deposited, and I was, indeed, the black hole of our family. (By the way, every dysfunctional family has one.) I had a way of sucking the joy out of everyone, and when they weren't bowing down and worshiping my dreams, my wants, and my desires, I would quickly become angry. Thanks be to God, He allowed me to see that life was not about me, and that true joy doesn't come by serving myself, but serving others. After all, Jesus did say, "*It is more blessed to give than to receive.*" (Acts 20:35)

HURT

Have you ever wondered why hurt people tend to hurt people? Did you know that many psychologists will tell you that the flip side of hurt is anger? Are you aware of the fact that those that are treated poorly early in life, often treat others the same throughout the rest of their life? Why is this the case? Well, I have a theory, and it goes something like what you are about to read.

Have you ever taken the time to pet a dog that, all of a sudden, snapped at you for touching a wound that was unknown to you? Actually, I think we all have. In fact, the underlying problem was not really with you, was it? The real problem was that, at some time or another, that seemingly harmless pet was probably run over by a car or the victim of an attack by another animal. Unbeknown to you, it was carrying around a wound that had never properly healed.

Some people are similar to a wounded dog. In other words, your relationship with them is fine until you do or say something that triggers painful feelings from their past. For example, you may know people that were constantly belittled by their siblings, parents, or their peers when they were growing up, and, consequently, they have developed a low opinion of themselves. People like this are sensitive to anyone that even hints they are dissatisfied with them in any way. They have developed the bad habit of FILTERING THE ACTIONS AND REACTIONS OF OTHERS THROUGH THEIR WOUNDED FEELINGS; therefore, they are sensitive to whatever may appear to be a cross look, lack of affection, or quick goodbye. If you close a phone conversation too quickly or forget to smile when they are around you, they are usually quick to react in a negative way. That is, they are quick to "snap at you." Of course, the problem is not really with you, is it? It is just that you happened to hit a wound that you were not aware of, and, if the truth be told, they are still harboring painful feelings from their past.

Some people, on the other hand, are so good at PROTECTING THEIR WOUND that they seldom give others a chance to TOUCH IT. They usually accomplish this by isolating themselves from those they might otherwise bless. They tend to shy away from social functions, and skittishly attend their local churches. They steer clear of jobs or positions of leadership that might bring back the painful feelings experienced years ago when they held similar positions. Though their actions are more passive in nature, they are, nonetheless, harmful in that they keep others from benefitting from their love, friendship, and God given talents.

Stay tuned: in the next chapter, we will see how to properly deal with wounded feelings in a biblical manner.

I'VE HAD IT

Many mothers are just plain worn out. They work fourteen to sixteen hour days, seven days a week, with little time to themselves. If you would ask them, working forty hours a week would seem like a part time job. Does this even come close to describing you? If so, then I believe you should pay close attention to what I am about to write.

Just as a well of water can only supply from an underground spring what it's FIRST BEING FED, a mother cannot expect to provide for her spouse and children what she is not first receiving from the Lord. No matter how hard she tries, she will eventually "come up dry" if she neglects to stay spiritually connected with the Lord. She will crack at the most inopportune time, and it is during these times that she will usually display her anger.

Colossians 1:8 states that the church at Colossae loved with a love that was not their own. We know this because Paul spoke of their "*love in the Spirit.*" Their love for others was not mustered or manmade. They were simply a channel through which God was able to work. Their souls were like bank accounts. Others could withdraw what God had deposited through the Spirit of God.

Every wife and mother reading this book is in the same position as the believers to whom Paul wrote. Your soul, your heart, and your emotions are like a bank account. If your husband, children, or in-laws try to withdraw more than God has been allowed to deposit, then they will get a "STATEMENT FROM THE BANK." However, this time, you will be the owner of the bank, and you will usually make that "statement" by crying, complaining, yelling, clamming up, or by distancing yourself from your loved ones. If your immediate family members are the constant recipients of such "statements," I would highly recommend that you take the following steps:

1. Recognize that mere desire alone is not enough to provide the love and care that your family needs.

    The second chapter of Exodus tells us of the time Moses killed an Egyptian that was beating one of the Israelites. As far as I can tell, Moses had a great motive. He was tired of the oppression that his native people were enduring, and, in his mind, it was high time to do something about it. But he acted alone in the matter, without the help of God. He acted in faith, but his faith was in himself.

    In the same way, I believe many mothers truly want to be patient, kind, and consistently loving toward their children and their spouses, but they lack one very important ingredient. That is the power and strength to accomplish what they truly want to do. Any mother that finds herself in this position must first realize her utter inability, in and of herself, to love her family the way they need to be loved. She is in dire need of a SOURCE OUTSIDE OF HERSELF; her underground spring. Jesus referred to this "underground spring" in John 7:37-38:

". . . If any man thirst, let him come unto me, and drink. He that believeth on me, as the scripture hath said, out of his belly shall flow rivers of living water."

2. Your spiritual condition before God must be of utmost importance.

In Mark 6:14-56 and Matthew 14:12-36, the Bible gives us a glimpse of about a twenty-four hour period in the life of Christ. During that day, the Bible tells us Jesus received word of the death of His cousin, John the Baptist, He welcomed His disciples back from their recent missionary trip and intently listened to their stories of what God had done, He organized a feast that fed thousands of people, He traveled by sea, He dealt with the hardness of the disciples' hearts, He instructed many in the way of the Lord—believe me, that is an exhausting task in and of itself, as some have rightly said, an hour of preaching is the equivalent to eight hours of manual labor—and last, but certainly not least, He performed an incredible amount of miracles.

Jesus had to have been physically, mentally, emotionally, and spiritually drained at the end of that particular day, however, I find it interesting that in the morning He seems to start all over again with the same amount of stamina as the day before. What kept Him going? When most people would have taken a few days to get their composure back, Jesus was at it again with the same level of intensity as the day before. I believe the answer can be found in Matthew 14:23:

"And when He had sent the multitudes away, He went up into a mountain apart to pray: and when the evening was come, he was there alone."

To me this is a very intriguing verse. I love it because it shows that in the midst of a horrendously busy day, Jesus found time to get alone with His Heavenly Father in prayer. In my mind, I have no doubt what was taking place in the heart and soul of Christ. He was giving time for His individual "well" to fill up with more love, joy, peace, wisdom, and strength, so that in the morning He would have the power and the spiritual ability to continue doing what He had so effectively accomplished the day before.

Like Jesus, you moms need to remember that the single most important event in your day is your time alone with the Lord through prayer and Bible reading. This is your time to get in touch with that "underground spring" that Jesus spoke of in the seventh chapter of John. This is your time to take a trip to the Bank of Heaven and allow God to deposit that which is necessary for you to be the godly wife and mother He desires you to be. REMEMBER, YOUR FAMILY DOES NOT SIMPLY NEED YOU, THEY NEED CHRIST, HIS LOVE, HIS JOY, AND HIS PEACE WITHIN YOU!

Husbands, it is also your responsibility to assist your wives in this task. I don't believe it is fair to criticize your wife for venting her frustrations (issuing a "STATEMENT") if you are not willing to help her have time alone with the Lord. If you see that your wife is caught up in a busy schedule, then you may need to take care of the breakfast duties, arrange for a babysitter to watch the children, or take the children off her hands by taking them to a park or playground.

DRIVING RECKLESSLY

After speaking on the subject of anger, I am often approached by parents that ask me what they can do to help their frequent angry outbursts. They are usually faithful Christians that have prayed about the very same issue. They have asked for forgiveness and Divine assistance on many occasions, but are still aware of that unholy fire that frequently flares up within them. Is God not hearing them? Are they failing to take hold of the promises of God? Not necessarily. Their hearts may be right and their intentions pure, yet if they are failing to properly bring their children under subjection, then they should not expect to feel any differently than they do when their children are acting in an unruly manner.

My wife and I love having children. The Lord has seen fit to give us four girly girls and one very boyish boy. (My wife's chromosomes must be a little stronger than mine.) Nevertheless, I will readily admit that children not in subjection to parental authority are not always pleasant to be around, and the first emotion that an unruly child spurs in a parent is usually anger.

What would you think of a reckless driver that frequently prayed for safety in his travels? Do you think that God would obligate Himself to answer his prayers? Should this person expect God to supernaturally intervene in his life when he is behind the wheel? I John 3:22 actually speaks to this end. Concerning prayer, John writes:

"And whatsoever we ask, we receive of him, BECAUSE WE KEEP HIS COMMANDMENTS, and do those things that are pleasing in His sight."

Clearly the Bible is teaching us that if our works do not line up with our faith, then we cannot expect our faith to "work" for us! As far as parenting is concerned, parents that continually pray for victory over their problem with anger must not expect God to mysteriously answer if they are not also willing to train their children in a practical way.

I have often said that we don't need child training seminars as much as we need parent training seminars. With that said, here are a few steps that should help you to stop "driving recklessly," and learn to become the parents that God desires you to be:

1. Sincerely and intentionally ask God to give you the wisdom that you need to parent effectively.

    James 1:5 tells us that God WILL give wisdom, discretion and understanding to those that earnestly ask in faith.
2. Don't settle for second best.

    Proverbs 29:17 promises: "*Correct thy son, and he shall give thee rest; yea, he shall give delight unto thy soul.*" This verse is just as much of a promise in the Word of God as John 3:16. Don't ever succumb to the idea that parenting has to be a hopeless and horrible experience. God's Word reveals otherwise.
3. Read good books and biblical materials.

Proverbs 11:14 teaches: *"... in the multitude of counselors there is safety."*

4. Work on your own spiritual character.

    I have come to the conclusion that good parenting is not just something that you do, it is more about who you are.

5. Find someone that has been successful in the area of parenting and converse with them on a regular basis.

    Proverbs 13:20 says: *"He that walketh with wise men shall be wise ..."*

UNTHANKFULNESS

Two miles per hour. That's how fast we were moving on the Pennsylvania Turnpike. In two and a half hours, I was scheduled to be in New Jersey to oversee a wedding rehearsal.

Many sighs and groans could be heard from the inside of our car. I was tense, frustrated, and on the verge of panic. I was convinced that when I stopped to pay my toll, I was going to protest having to pay eleven dollars to supposedly "zip" across the state.

Finally, it was over. The cars ahead began to move faster, and we could see what was causing the big holdup. A car had collided with the railing and flipped over into the middle of the highway. From my meager perspective, there was no way the driver could have survived. The car AND the driver were totaled. Suddenly my tardiness seemed like a very small problem. Right then I asked God to forgive me, and my spirit of anger was replaced by a spirit of compassion as I realized I had much to be thankful for.

We can analyze this thing called anger over and over again, but many times I think we just need a good dose of thankfulness to cure this spiritual sickness. The employee that is always complaining about the extra hours he has to work may need to start thanking God that he even has a job. The wife that is frequently frustrated at her husband's tardiness at the dinner table may need to start thanking the Lord that her husband is working so hard for the family. Church members that have developed a negative attitude about their churches and pastors may need to take the time to remember that the worst day in church is better than the best day in a lost, unconverted state.

UNREALISTIC EXPECTATIONS

I love Proverbs 14:4. This incredibly simple, yet profound verse says:

"Where no oxen are, the crib is clean: but much increase is by the strength of the ox."

Not to be crude, but this proverb is teaching that the poor farmer with little or no cattle also has a minimal amount of "dirty work" to do in his barn. The prosperous farmer, on the other hand, that possesses a good number of cattle and other farm animals will have the never ending job of removing waste.

Now that we have had a little lesson in farming, let's ask ourselves why this verse is even in the Bible? I believe the answer is simple. God is teaching us that the individual or the organization that is constantly moving forward and forever reaching its goals should expect to have a lot of "dirty work" to perform. Unlike the individual or the company that sees little growth and success, there are employees that need to be reprimanded, budgets that have to be balanced, money that has to be accounted for, and certain levels of success that must be sustained.

One of the biggest breakthroughs of my ministry came when I just accepted the fact that life is hard, people are tough to deal with, and any task that is worthwhile is going to be difficult to accomplish. I realized that I had a choice to make on a daily basis. Was I going to live with tightness in my chest, knots in my stomach, and a perturbed spirit, or would I patiently endure the little daily crosses that I am expected to bear? From that point on, I stopped allowing my joy and contentment to be like a yo-yo tied to a string called circumstance. My spirit was now much more stable; therefore, my ability to effectively accomplish what God called me to do was greatly enhanced.

Problems are not always a sign of failure. Sometimes they are a sign of success. So, if the shoe fits, then I recommend the following bit of advice:

> "Stop complaining, grab a shovel, and be thankful that you even have enough cattle to make such a mess!"

YOURSELF

It's a rather popular story. David saw Bathsheeba, David sinned with Bathsheeba, and in order to cover up his sin, he arranged for the murder of Urijah, Bathsheeba's husband. In time the Lord sent the prophet Nathan to confront the king, and shortly thereafter David repented of the sin that he had committed with Bathsheeba.

During the confrontation between Nathan and King David, David had a very intriguing reaction. Look closely at the response of the king after he was approached by Nathan:

II Samuel 12: 1-7: *"And the Lord sent Nathan unto David. And he came unto him, and said unto him, 'There were two men in one city; the one rich, and the other poor. The rich man had exceeding many flocks and herds: But the poor man had nothing, save one little ewe lamb, which he had bought and nourished up: and it grew up together with him, and with his children; it did eat of his own meat, and drank of his own cup, and lay in his bosom, and was unto him as a daughter.*

'And there came a traveler unto the rich man, and he spared to take of his own flock and of his own herd, to dress for the wayfaring man that was come unto him; but took the poor man's lamb, and dressed it for the man that was come to him.

AND DAVID'S ANGER WAS GREATLY KINDLED AGAINST THE MAN; and he said to Nathan, 'As the Lord liveth, the man that hath done this thing shall surely die: And he shall restore the lamb fourfold, because he

did this thing, and because he had no pity.'
And Nathan said to David, 'Thou art the man."

If you are familiar with this story, then you know the reason Nathan told this narrative to David. Using a simple illustration, Nathan was comparing King David to the rich man that possessed "many flocks and herds." Just as the wealthy man displayed his selfishness by taking the poor man's lamb, David also acted in a similar manner by taking Bathsheeba unto himself.

From observation AND from personal experience, I am convinced that we do not like to see our own shortcomings and mistakes in other people. I believe this story bears out this concept. David's anger was "greatly kindled" because, subconsciously, Nathan's story reminded David of himself.

Have you ever wondered why the "odd man out" in a group of children is usually the first to pick on another child that has a low rank in the pecking order at school? In many cases his desire to ridicule is fueled by his subconscious disdain for his own feelings of rejection and awkwardness. Did you know it is a common occurrence for pastors that have fallen into heinous sin to have preached in an unusually adamant manner about the very same sin weeks or months before they are exposed? This sounds kind of weird, doesn't it? However, we must remember that, in Jeremiah 17:9, God described the human heart by saying, *"The heart is deceitful above all things, and desperately wicked: who can know it."*

The next time you find yourself annoyed with other people, ask yourself why. It could be that you are keenly aware of their mishaps only because you've had, or are having, a deep inner struggle in that particular area yourself. It could be that their lives are simply a mirror of your own, and you are not very pleased with what you see.

Chapter Eight

MAKING PROGRESS

IT'S POSSIBLE

Jerry Bridges, in his book, The Pursuit of Holiness, wrote:

> "Only one who has a strong desire to be holy will ever persevere in the painfully slow and difficult task of pursuing holiness." (2)

Painful. Difficult. Slow. Most of us readily receive words like victory, breakthrough, overcome, restoration, and renewal, but words like painful, difficult, and slow, are not very

Angry Without a Cause

appealing descriptions, are they?

My natural side would like to give every one of you that struggles with anger ten easy steps that will work within 24 hours. The underlying difficulty with this is that God has not provided any such remedy. He has, however, started with the promise that consistent victory over the sins that continually beat you down is ENTIRELY POSSIBLE.

Ephesians 4:31 commands us to forsake "*all bitterness, and wrath, and anger . . .*" Consider this! Would God give us a command that is impossible to keep? In my opinion that would be form of spiritual torture.

Also, let's consider Galatians 5:22-23. These verses talk explicitly about the fruits of the Holy Spirit. Just as an apple tree is to produce apples and an orange tree has been designed to bear oranges, every Christian is expected to produce the fruits of the Holy Spirit. These fruits are love, joy, peace, longsuffering (patience), gentleness, goodness, faith, meekness, and TEMPERANCE.

I get excited about the word temperance. It

literally means to have self-control. I guess my excitement is due to the fact that without Christ I don't have a whole lot of self-discipline. My parents, my former college buddies, and my wife can all attest to that. I'm actually a "basket case" without the Holy Spirit, and that has been one of the main reasons I have clung so close to Christ since my conversion.

In regards to the issue of anger, the need is not for you to have more will-power, but more Supernatural power. You must come to the point where you realize that serving Christ isn't hard; it's impossible without the aid of the Holy Spirit. Herein lies what I believe to be the fundamental difference between modern psychology and Christianity. Psychology can sometimes give you the right things to do, but it can NEVER GIVE YOU THE POWER TO DO THOSE THINGS. Many thanks be to God for not only telling us what to do, but giving us the ability to be obedient unto Him. Praise God!

There seems to be a good number of songs sung and testimonies given in the church that make much of the Christian's victory over the penalty of sin. That's all wonderful and biblical at the same time; however, when God sent Jesus to the earth, He had more in mind than just getting us into Heaven. He also sent Christ so that WE could reveal a little bit of Heaven on earth through lives pleasing to Him. Here are a few verses in the New Testament that reveal this awesome truth:

> II Corinthians 5:14-15: *"For the love of Christ constraineth us; because we thus judge, that if one died for all, then were all dead: AND THAT HE DIED FOR ALL, THAT THEY WHICH LIVE SHOULD NOT HENCEFORTH LIVE UNTO THEMSELVES, but unto Him which died for them, and rose again."*

> I Peter 2:24: *"Who [Christ] His own self bare our sins in His body on the tree [cross], that we, being dead to sins, SHOULD LIVE UNTO RIGHTEOUSNESS . . ."*

Titus 2:14: *"Who [Christ] gave Himself for us, that He might redeem [deliver] us from all iniquity, and PURIFY UNTO HIMSELF a peculiar people, zealous of good works."*

This entire chapter has been designed to give you some pro-active measures to effectively deal with anger, but before we go further it must be understood that God has made a way for you to be set free from the sins in your life that so quickly hurt your testimony, and your confidence toward God and others around you.

LIVE FOR GOD

The best preventative medicine a person can take to maintain a calm and a patient spirit is to diligently seek after the Lord and walk in obedience to His Word. Too simplistic? I don't think so. Let's face it. Those that do not live a life that is pleasing to the Lord are opening themselves to SITUATIONS, FEELINGS, AND BROKEN RELATIONSHIPS, that will, time and again, tempt them to possess a spirit of anger. For example, a person that has not learned to sacrificially love others on a daily basis will often experience a greater amount of needless strife and confrontation in their lives in comparison to someone that consistently displays the love of Christ to others. Also, people lacking faith in God will often become either emotionally, physically, or verbally hostile in a crunch situation. Whereas the individual that has learned to trust God in every situation will not be as emotionally volatile in a "tight spot."

Have you fought a lifelong battle with anger? Have you tried counting to ten, thinking happy thoughts, or even medication in order to remedy your problem? It could just be that you need to apply biblical principles to your everyday life to AVOID many of the situations that so often tempt you to lose your cool. There is a good chance that instead of fighting this temptation, God's will is for you to learn to avoid "anger traps" as much as is possible by living a life that is pleasing to Him.

I once had a manager that came to me and

heatedly said, "How come you ordered the black side-sills for that customer's car?"

By God's grace, I calmly said, "Because I really don't know much about this business and I have a lot to learn."

You should have seen it. It was as if the wind was taken right out of his sail. Instead of answering with the typical, defensive remark, I was able to respond in a humble manner. My manager's retort melted into a sheepish reply: "Well, just remember not to do that again."

I had a decision to make when my boss initially came into me. Was I going to allow myself to end up in a heated argument and then ask God to help me to control my temper AFTER I WAS ALREADY EMOTIONALLY INVOLVED in the situation, or was I going to answer him in a humble manner, and thereby AVOID an argument altogether? Thanks be to God, by walking in obedience to the Lord, I was able to avoid a situation that would have tempted me to lose my testimony and my ability to witness to him at a later time.

Are you walking with God? Do you read your Bible habitually? On Sundays, can you be found darkening the doors of a biblical church? Have you taken the time to learn to walk in the Spirit, and thereby portray a spirit of love, joy, gentleness, and self-control in your life? If not, then I firmly believe YOU WILL BE AFFORDED MORE OPPORTUNITIES TO LOSE YOUR TEMPER THAN THE DEDICATED CHRISTIAN THAT SEEKS TO FOLLOW THE LORD. Selfless people that are filled with God's love, joy, peace, and wisdom are usually very patient people; however, selfish people that are full of themselves and an unbelieving attitude are often angry, hotheaded individuals that are quick to blow up, and eventually blow out!

MAINTAIN AN ACCURATE VIEW OF YOURSELF

One afternoon I was sitting in my van at a busy intersection. While my children were in the back, listening to a children's tape, I heard the sound of rhythmic clamor, mixed with profanity, coming through the windows of our van. I rolled down my window and sternly said, "Hey buddy! Can you turn it down? My children don't need to hear all of that."

A few moments later, I heard a little voice in my head say something like, "Self, a few short years ago, that was you, a clueless teenager with a rusted out car and a premium sound system. You had no regard for God, and you could have cared less about the amount of curse words in your music."

I knew what I said to the young man was entirely appropriate, but after that conversation with myself, I was sure it was the tone of my voice and the spirit in which I spoke that was causing a spirit of conviction in my heart.

In Titus 3:2 the Apostle Paul told us that we are to *"speak evil of no man, to be no brawlers, but gentle, shewing all meekness unto all men."* In verse three Paul gives us a great reason why every Christian should be so willing to obey this command:

"For we ourselves also were sometimes foolish, disobedient, deceived, serving divers lusts and pleasures, living in malice and envy, hateful, and hating one another."

Simply put, Paul is teaching us that an understanding of what we would be, apart from the grace of God, should inspire us to be more patient toward those that have apparent spiritual and moral problems.

I am convinced that critical people HAVE NEVER TRULY SEEN HOW SPIRITUALLY BANKRUPT THEY ARE. They have spent much of their life looking down at others in order to experience an exalted view of themselves, and they are ignorant of the fact that often THEIR PRIDE IS SIMPLY A LADDER UPON WHICH THEIR ANGER CLIMBS.

They are two things taking place inside of me the longer I serve the Lord. First of all, I have fewer convictions and more preferences. Secondly, I am increasingly more understanding and patient toward those that struggle in certain areas.

I have made many mistakes in my life. In fact, I believe that I have made more bad decisions than good. Some have said of my teachings, "He has great insight." I say, "I've got great ME-SIGHT." I think I'm good at preaching on the subject of sin because it's one area where I can actually say I'm an expert. That being said, I guess I tend to be more patient toward others because I see so much of myself in them. TO CRITICIZE THEM WOULD BE TO CRITICIZE MYSELF.

Most critical people do not seem to realize that when they continually mock, ridicule, and look down on others, they are condemning themselves. Romans 2:1 deals with this idea:

> *"Therefore thou art inexcusable, O man, whosoever thou art that judgest: for wherein thou judgest another, thou condemnest thyself . . ."*

FAITH IN GOD

What kind of message are we sending to those around us when we throw something across the room, scream at the top of our lungs, or raise our hands in desperation? Are we portraying that our faith is resting in the Wonderful God of the Universe? Are we, by our actions and reactions, sending out the message that our Immutable (Unchanging), Omniscient (All-Knowing), and All-Powerful God is in complete control?

God has not promised everything that comes into the lives of His children will be good. But He has promised everything that He allows into our lives will work for His glory and, as a result, our eternal good. This truth is more than evident in Romans 8:28 where God says that "*. . . all things work together for good to them that love God, to them who are the called according to his purpose.*" AN INABILITY TO APPLY THIS PROMISE TO EVERYDAY EVENTS WILL CAUSE A PERSON TO EXPERIENCE NEEDLESS TIMES OF FRUSTRATION AND FRAZZLED NERVES.

I once heard a story of an older preacher that was praying with a novice pastor. The young pastor was surprised to hear his elder praying a prayer that went something like this:

> "Lord, I hate butter. Lord, I hate salt. And Lord, you know I hate baking powder."

By this time, the young pastor was quite perplexed, until the older pastor ended his prayer by saying, ". . . but I sure do love hot biscuits!"

Troublesome times and problematic people are typically God's ingredients to make us the mature children of God that He so desires us to be. Although these ingredients are not necessarily tasteful to us at the time, they tend to yield the peaceable fruit of righteousness in our lives. The child of God that recognizes this will be far less likely to become incensed by every negative situation that pops into his life.

In one of my pastorates, I was told by the pulpit committee that after serving the church for six months I would receive a pay raise. During those six months, our church grew rapidly and many changes occurred. After the six month period was over, I was approached by the head deacon about my potential pay raise. Even though I could have used the money, I felt it was not necessary to introduce another change to the people at that time.

To make a long story short, I put the ministry before my own financial needs again, and was going to have to bear the hard repercussions of my choice. For a moment I had a little pity party with me, myself, and I. Ironically, a few months later, I would understand why the Lord had not allowed the pay raise to occur.

About three months after rejecting my own pay hike, my wife and I found a beautiful house for sale. The home had my wife's name written all over it. The only problem is, we were sure we couldn't afford the payments. Thankfully, we were told by our realtor that we could possibly qualify for a special first-time buyer program offered by the state. We made our way to the bank to talk to the loan officer, and were notified that we barely qualified for the program! In fact, if we had made just $15.38 more per week, we wouldn't have qualified for the incredibly low interest rate that we received. Our decision to reject the increase in pay allowed us to live in the nicest house that we had ever occupied. I sure do love hot biscuits!!!

SLOW DOWN

I have been a Christian for sixteen years. I habitually read my Bible. I love my family. I pray, fast (I better be careful, I'm starting to sound like a Pharisee), and attend church regularly. Even so, if I get horrendously busy, I'm still tempted to get annoyed at anyone (as I stated in the last chapter) that becomes a HUMAN SPEED BUMP in my path.

May I ask you a question? Which is easier to stop: a car traveling ten miles per hour or a car traveling seventy-five miles per hour? Which one will produce MORE FRICTION when it's forced to come to a screeching halt? What's more, if a collision occurs, which one will cause more DAMAGE to the OBSTACLES that it runs into?

At times in our marriage, my "car" has been traveling seventy-five miles per hour. Consequently, from time to time, I have had the tendency to view my wife and my family as mere speed bumps or obstacles in my path to success. Thanks be to God that He has slowly seen fit to teach me that my wife and children are not just obstacles in my quest to win in life, but actually the prize!

How fast is your "car" traveling? Do you often find yourself running over your spouse, your children, your co-workers, and your friends? Are their backs full of "tread marks" from your emotional outbursts and unexpected tantrums? If so, you may need to start slowing down and stop traveling at such a hectic pace.

FORGIVENESS

One of the key factors to experiencing healing from deep emotional wounds and the anger that often results from them is forgiveness. Paul touched on this principle in his letter to the church in Ephesus. In Ephesians 4:31-32, Paul wrote:

"Let all bitterness, and wrath, and ANGER, and clamour, and evil speaking . . . be put away from you . . . and be ye kind one to another, tenderhearted, FORGIVING ONE ANOTHER, even as God for Christ's sake hath forgiven you."

Do you like to read those cute little statements that churches put on their signs? I know; some are kind of corny, but I must admit that others have been a great source of sermon fodder for me. On one occasion this is what I saw in front of a church as I was speeding by:

> "Forgiveness is letting the prisoner go, and realizing that, all along, the real prisoner was you."

When people fail to forgive those that have harmed them, they are opting to hold on to hurt feelings, and, quite frankly, those feelings will eventually cause them to live in an emotionally imprisoned state. Anger, bitterness, fear, and pessimism will be the bars that hold them captive. Unless they learn to forgive their perpetrator, they will allow that very same person to victimize them twice. Once, when the initial crime takes place, and again as they live lives tormented by their feelings of contempt for anyone and everything that reminds them of their painful past.

Forgiveness is giving up the right to be mad, get even, or maintain a spirit of bitterness toward someone that has violated you. When God forgave us, He gave up His right to punish us for violating His law. He gave up the right to carry out Divine justice upon our lives. The problem is that PEOPLE WHO NEGLECT TO FORGIVE

THOSE THAT HAVE HURT THEM, ARE OFTEN PUNISHING THOSE THAT ARE CLOSEST TO THEM IN THE PRESENT FOR THE VERY SAME INJUSTICES.

All over the world, there are ex-church members that, at one time or another, were hurt by one of their former pastors or fellow members. Though their wounds were received in the PAST, in an odd sort of way, they are now punishing themselves and the churches that they skittishly attend by withholding their allegiance, talents, resources, and affections from the rest of the body. Although they have much to offer other believers, their inner defense mechanisms will not allow them to be thrust into another situation where they might be hurt again.

By the way, it seems that for the past thirty or forty years, pastors have been doing all they can to paint a beautiful picture of Christianity, so the world will be attracted to it. But Jesus did not use this as His primary method for promoting Christianity. In Mark 8:34-38 and Luke 14:25-27, Jesus forthrightly taught that

Christianity is characterized by a cross. Do you know what a cross was used for in biblical times? It was an instrument of capital punishment. In Bible times, people's minds were not full of thoughts of ornate buildings and old fashioned songs when Jesus mentioned the cross. Instead, they thought of a method of punishment that produced a tremendous amount of shame, humiliation, pain, and agony.

I would like to say something that we need to say more in the church at large. SOMETIMES, CHRISTIANITY HURTS, and people (even Christians) are often the source of that pain. I certainly do not mean to come across as harsh or insensitive, but some people just need to get over the fact that they have been violated and mistreated by other people. Crosses hurt, and if you are going to follow Christ, you had better realize that following Christ can sometimes be a painful experience.

I have also observed that there are many church leaders, owners of businesses, managers, and supervisors that seem to be punishing those under their authority for the relational crimes committed against them early in their careers. These leaders are often standoffish, overly negative, and devoid of vision. They have not only lost their faith in God, but also in people. Their expectations are low and no young visionary is going to change their minds. They will just not allow disappointment to have another shot at knocking them down. Leaders in this position will find that a spirit of forgiveness and some simple changes in thought processes will help them make tremendous progress in this area.

Before I end this section, I would like to clarify that when God gave up the right to punish us for our sins, it was not that He just looked the other way and nonchalantly allowed us to enter into His family. Actually, before He could forgive us and give up the right to punish us, He had to allow His only Son, Jesus Christ, to be punished for our sins. Now, those that repent and turn to Christ by faith are forgiven of all their sins that they have ever committed.

By the way, aren't you glad that God forgives

you every time you sin? Aren't you glad that God forgives you no matter how grievous your sin is in His sight? Aren't you glad that God forgives you no matter how often you commit the same sin over and over again? If so, then we should also be willing to forgive others in the same way.

KEEP YOUR EARS OPEN

Stephen Covey, in his book, 7 Habits of Highly Effective People, lists the following as one of his seven habits:

> "Seek first to understand and then to be understood" (3)

James, one of the writers of the New Testament, said it like this:

James 1:19: *". . . let every man be swift to hear, slow to speak, slow to wrath:"*

Not long ago I was attempting to sneak Christmas gifts into our home. I quietly made my way through the front door and the living room. Tip-toeing, I then proceeded into the kitchen and eventually arrived in the bedroom. I was proud of myself. I had traveled all the way through a house occupied by seven people without being noticed. Or so I thought. As I was putting presents away in the bedroom, I saw a pair of eyes peering though the crack between the door and the door jam. I was under surveillance.

As a Dad, I was thrown into panic. It was a parent's worst nightmare (kind-of). My oldest son, Mark, was gazing at the Christmas presents that we had purchased for the children, and I feared the element of surprise was now taken away from the "big day."

I went to the door and said in a stern voice, "Mark, this is unacceptable. You know you're not to follow anyone that looks like they are trying to hide Christmas gifts [In my defense, we had just talked about this the day before], and you're definitely not supposed to spy on your parents when they're unpacking presents." (At this time I'm sure I started sounding like many parents in situations like this; like Charlie Brown's teacher. I think it's spelled something like this: "Wa-womp wa-womp wa-womp womp womp!") I sent him to his room and quickly shut the door; however, I was completely unaware of the fact that in a few moments I would be eating a big piece of "humble pie."

About ten minutes later, I went to talk to Mark. To my dismay, I discovered that he had been Christmas shopping that morning. He was only following me to my room because that was the place he chose to hide my Christmas gift. It didn't take me long to realize that I was not acting like a highly effective parent. I didn't listen before I spoke. I didn't "seek first to understand and then to be understood." The tension caused that day could have been avoided if I had taken the time to open my ears before I opened my mouth.

BE UP-FRONT

Naturally, there are three types of people when it comes to handling conflict and dealing with difficulties. Some run straight into their problems without much forethought of the aftermath that may follow, while others are perfectly happy running away from their problems. Then there are those that are content to run with their problems. Which one are you? If you would, put your thinking-cap on, and take some time to psychoanalyze yourself. Just remember, the longer you take, the more money you'll have to charge yourself.

How do you react when your friends, family, or acquaintances ask or expect something of you that causes you to feel uncomfortable or violated in some way? Are you apt to respond in an abrupt fashion? Are you the kind of person that has to fight against the temptation to roar like a lion in the face your opposition? If so, then you are definitely the type that tends to run straight into a problem.

You may be the kind of person that handles conflict by running away from it. You get just as annoyed as those mentioned in the last paragraph, but you respond in an entirely different manner. Instead of expressing your anger, you tend to suppress it. In turn, this causes you to stop answering the phone when that certain someone calls to talk with you. When you know they might be dropping in, you conveniently leave so that you are not forced to face the issue. One of the problems associated with behavior such as this is you can only suppress your feelings for so long. The time will come when you express them at a very inopportune time.

Maybe it is your style to put up with a problem or problematic person in order to keep from dealing with any type of conflict at all. People like this are usually afraid of confrontation, and consequently tend to compromise their core beliefs in order to appease others. As before, they get just as aggravated as the people mentioned in the last two paragraphs, but they do not seem to have the intestinal fortitude (guts) to take decisive action. If this describes you, then you're probably the type that runs with a problem.

So, how should a person handle it when they are faced with an issue that tests their people skills? How should they respond? Should they run into, away, or with the situation? The answer is actually very simple, yet entirely biblical. Solomon touched on this subject many years ago when he wrote what we know to be Proverbs 27:5-6:

"Open rebuke is better than secret love. Faithful are the wounds of a friend; but the kisses of an enemy are deceitful."

This verse could be the syllabus for a class titled, "Conflict Resolution." The verse teaches that we all have a biblical responsibility to be open, transparent, and truthful with others, even when disagreements arise. God is teaching us that the proper way to handle conflict involves speaking in a truthful and forthright manner, yet always with a spirit of love.

As a father I am faced with situations that test

my ability to be up-front and truthful with others. For example, from time to time, I am approached by a parent asking if my children may watch a taboo TV show or participate in something that would not normally be approved. In such instances I have a few options to choose from. I can respond in an abrupt manner and cause a needless amount of tension (run straight into the problem), I can attempt to avoid any further situations that involve that particular parent and thereby cause them to feel awkward or rejected (run away from the problem), I can go along with their request and complain to someone else about that parent at a later time (run with the problem), or I can calmly and methodically ESTABLISH VERBAL BOUNDARIES, (be up-front).

As a Christian, I have a biblical responsibility to speak the truth in love. When I am in the "hot seat," and a parent is standing in front of me, waiting an answer, I am acting in a way that is less than biblical if I do not calmly respond to them by saying something like:

"As a family, we like to stick with lower rated movies for the children. Would you have another video that they could watch?"

Or:

"Thank you for inviting my child to spend the night with your son/daughter; however, we have a family rule that would not allow that to happen. Could we plan to have your entire family over for a barbecue this Saturday?"

At this point, I leave the friendship (or the potential friendship) in their hands. They may choose to work with our belief system, or they can choose to act in an offended manner. The quality of their Christianity and their maturity level in Christ is usually revealed by their response.

To alleviate underlying feelings of frustration and ongoing times of tension, you must be open and transparent with others and learn to draw VERBAL BOUNDARIES in a calm and confident manner. The only other option is to bully your way through a problem with abusive language or emotional outbursts, or you can always suppress your emotions until you, at a later time, express your frustrations through gossip sessions, snide remarks, sarcasm, cold stares, or strained communications.

BE PATIENT

After reading the title to this section, you may be thinking something like, "Be patient? Can you give me something a little deeper than that to help me overcome my problem with anger?" Actually, I'm not speaking of your ability to tolerate the shortcomings of others, as much as those of your own.

In my last pastorate, I had the privilege of overseeing the spiritual lives of many first-generation Christians. I love first-generation Christians. Generally speaking, they tend to be very zealous and incredibly trainable. All that being said, because of their great zeal for the Lord, they would often grow impatient with their rate of growth in Christ. This is what I call a good problem. At least, it is until it becomes a source of discouragement.

One of the verses that I would often share with my people through my sermons and one-on-one conversations was Proverbs 24:16. Surprisingly, it says:

"For a JUST man FALLETH seven times, and riseth up again: but the wicked shall fall into mischief."

The moral of the story: from time to time, even godly people "blow it." The primary difference is that they are not comfortable living with any amount of known sin in their lives. They do fall down, but, by God's grace, they consistently get up.

Please remember that consistent victory over anger is entirely possible, but it may not happen overnight. In your attempts to win over anger, be patient with yourself as well as others. Just be sure you do not grow complacent!

Chapter 9

Dealing With an Angry Person

YOUR INTRINSIC VALUE

As I stated earlier, people tend to believe they are as low and insignificant as they feel when others are angry at them. In fact, only a few resolute individuals with an abnormal amount of resolve are able to endure a gauntlet of ridicule and scorn without being negatively affected. I have written this next section for those with a view of themselves formed in light of the way others have woefully treated them.

When you go shopping, how do you determine

the value of a particular item? Obviously, you do this by looking at the price tag. Likewise, every reader must understand that, figuratively speaking, there is a price tag attached to their soul, and written on that tag are the words, "The life of the Son of God." John 3:16, the most popular verse of the Bible, bears this out. With a receptive heart, read the following verse:

> John 3:16: *"For God so loved the world, that HE GAVE His only begotten Son, that whosoever believeth in Him should not perish, but have everlasting life."*

If I was to take a piece of gold and throw it into a mud puddle, would you still want it if I offered it to you? What if I took the same nugget and smashed it against a wall? Would you still be interested in it? Of course, the answer is yes. The reason is very simple, yet entirely applicable to the subject at hand. Whether I throw a piece of gold into mud or smash it against a brick wall, it still maintains its INTRINSIC VALUE. In the same way, no matter how poorly you have been treated by others, in God's sight, you still have intrinsic value. You can assess that value by looking at the price that God paid to redeem you when Christ died on the cross.

Before I delve any deeper into this section, I have a confession to make. I am not a very secure person, at least, not in and of myself. If the truth be told, not too many people are. Naturally, most struggle with feelings of fear, inferiority, and inadequacy. To compensate for this inner dilemma, most people trust in something to help them deal with their feelings of inadequacy. Sports, money, looks, automobiles, houses, peers, jobs, and male-female relationships are among the top sellers. However, some are also using their children, grandchildren, or even their prominence in religious circles to improve their own sense of worthiness.

I'm so glad that my value does not rely upon any of the things mentioned above. My significance does not rest in my looks, my waistline (it's a good thing), nor my accomplishments in life. I am not a "somebody" because I have done the same as, or more than, another body. I am only valuable because God has deemed me so!

Romans 12:3 tells us that we are not to think of ourselves more highly than we ought. To violate this principle would be to involve ourselves in what the Bible refers to as pride. On the other hand, I believe that it is also an insult to God's creativity for one to possess a LESS THAN ACCURATE view of themselves based upon the angry looks and spiteful words of their spouses, parents, siblings, or peers. A person in this position should take some time to realize that their value must not be determined by the actions and attitudes of others, but by the Manufacturer and the Purchaser of their soul.

Supplies must have been low—there is only one of you to go around—and demand must have been high—look at the expensive payment that God made for you—the day Christ died for you. This Divine act of love caused your value to literally "shoot through the roof." Now it is time for you to "buy in" on the deal and come to grips with the real value of your soul.

NO RESPECTER OF PERSONS

It wasn't long ago that I would find myself taking the snide remarks and angry outbursts of others far too personally. Looking back, many sleepless nights could have been avoided if I would have only had the understanding that ANGER IS NO RESPECTER OF PERSONS. In other words, angry people are generally angry at whomever or whatever gets in their way. The problem is not, therefore, always with the unfortunate individual that has triggered the irrational behavior. In reality, the trigger is cocked and the gun is loaded long before the first shot is ever fired.

In Matthew 5:44, Jesus said:

". . . Love your enemies, bless them that curse you, do good to them that hate you, and pray for them which despitefully use you, and persecute you."

Although this is one of the more difficult verses for a child of God to obey, it becomes increasingly more challenging when we personalize many of the abrupt statements and the stern looks that we receive from others. Please remember, when you cross paths with people that often "blow their tops," you are much like an archeologist. You did not make the artifact, you merely discovered it.

P.S. I really think that when we find ourselves absolutely furious at the critical words and the judgmental looks of others, it is because, deep down inside, we fear that their words and thoughts concerning us may ring with a little bit of truth. In other words, we are often upset because we are scared that their opinion of us may be more accurate than we care to admit. Nevertheless, a proper understanding of the fact that angry people are typically angry at whatever or whomever keeps them from getting what they want, should help everyone of us to stop taking the irrational behavior of others in a personal way. Remember it's hardly ever about you! Their problem with anger is usually a manifestation of a deeper problem that they have within themselves.

For more information about
Hitting Home, go to
www.HelpwithAnger.com.

To inquire about having
Dr. Raymond Force to speak at your
next event, go to
www.ChristianMarriageSpeaker.com
or
www.YourChristianSpeaker.org.

BIBLIOGRAPHY

All scripture quotations have been taken from the King James Version of the Holy Bible.

1. *Changing Your Husband by Faith*, Sermon by Pastor James MacDonald
2. *The Pursuit of Holiness*, Jerry Bridges
3. *7 Habits of Highly Effective People,* Stephen Covey